bright spark

brilliant brain

cool kid

superstar

great work

amazing work

I Can Learn

Reading

Written by Brenda Apsley

Illustrated by John Haslam

This book belongs to

Thea B

EGMONT

 # Tips for happy home learning

Make learning fun by working at your child's pace
and always giving tasks which s/he can do.
Tasks that are too difficult will discourage
her/him from trying again.

Give encouragement and praise and remember
to award gold stars and sticker badges for
effort as well as good work.

Always do too little rather than too much,
and finish each session on a positive note.

Don't work when you or your child
is tired or hungry.

Reinforce workbook activities and new ideas by
making use of real objects around the home.

EGMONT

We bring stories to life

Published in Great Britain by Egmont Books Limited,
239 Kensington High Street, London W8 6SA
www.egmont.co.uk

Printed in Italy.
ISBN 1 4052 1560 7
4 6 8 10 9 7 5 3

Read the sentences. Draw lines under the words that will finish them. Write the words in the boxes.

I am a _____ .	boy	by	girl
I am _____ .	five	seven	six
I live in a _____ .	house	horse	flat
My mum is a _____ .	man	woman	worm
My dad is a _____ .	boy	man	map

Here is a happy face. Draw lines from the words to the parts of the face. The first one is done to show you how.

eye

hair

ear

teeth

nose

mouth

lips

chin

Read the number words. Draw a line from the number word to the number of rabbits in each burrow.

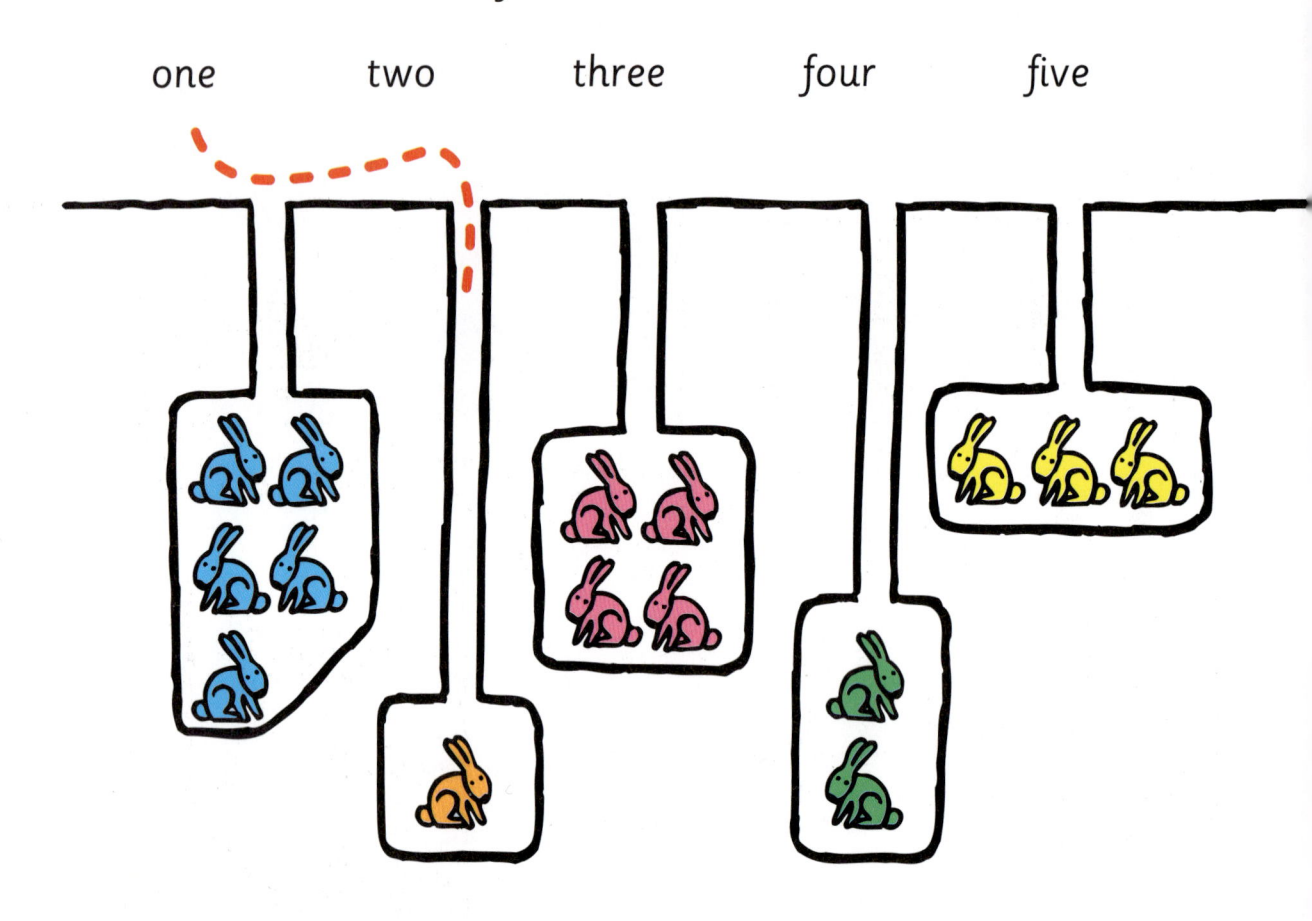

one   two   three   four   five

Now write the numeral for each number word. The first one has been done for you.

one	1	six	
two		seven	
three		eight	
four		nine	
five		ten	

8
4
2
1
5   7
9
3
6
10

 How many blue rabbits are there?

six   seven   eight   nine   ten

Here is a rhyme. Some of the number words are missing. Choose the number words from the list, and write them in the boxes.

One, two, [   ] , four, [   ] ,

Once I caught a fish alive.

Six, [   ] , eight, [   ] , [   ] ,

Then I let it go again.

ten

seven

three

nine

five

Note for parents: Write numerals 1 to 10 and number words one to ten on pieces of paper for a matching game to play.

Read the weather words.
Draw lines to match them to the pictures.

wind

sun

cloud

rain

snow

Answer these questions about the weather.
Tick **yes** or **no**.

Is rain wet?   yes [ ]   no [ ]

Is it hot on a sunny day?   yes [ ]   no [ ]

Is snow dry?   yes [ ]   no [ ]

Look outside. What is the weather like today?
Draw a picture and write a weather word for today.

Today is [ ]

 What is your favourite sort of weather?

Read this story. The Wind and the Sun.

The wind said he was stronger than the sun.
The sun did not agree.

The one who could make the man take off his coat would be the strongest.

The wind blew hard. The wind made the man feel cold. He pulled his coat around him.

The sun shone on the man.
The sun made him hot.
The man took off his coat. The sun said he was the strongest.

Tick the correct answer.

Did the wind make the man hot?   yes ☐   no ☐

Did the sun make the man hot?   yes ☐   no ☐

Who made the man take off his coat, the sun or the wind?   sun ☐   wind ☐

Note for parents: Look at a weather map in a newspaper to show your child what the weather will be like where you live.

8 Colours

Read the colour words.

blue   red   green   yellow   white   black

The colour words are missing in these sentences.
Choose the correct colour words, and write them in the boxes.

Frogs are [   ] .   white

Snow is [   ] .   yellow

Bananas are [   ] .   red

A fire engine is [   ] .   black

Coal is [   ] .   green

COAL

Colour the picture.

You have really brightened up the page!

Here's a picture I made using sticky paper shapes. Match the shape word to the shapes in the picture by drawing lines.

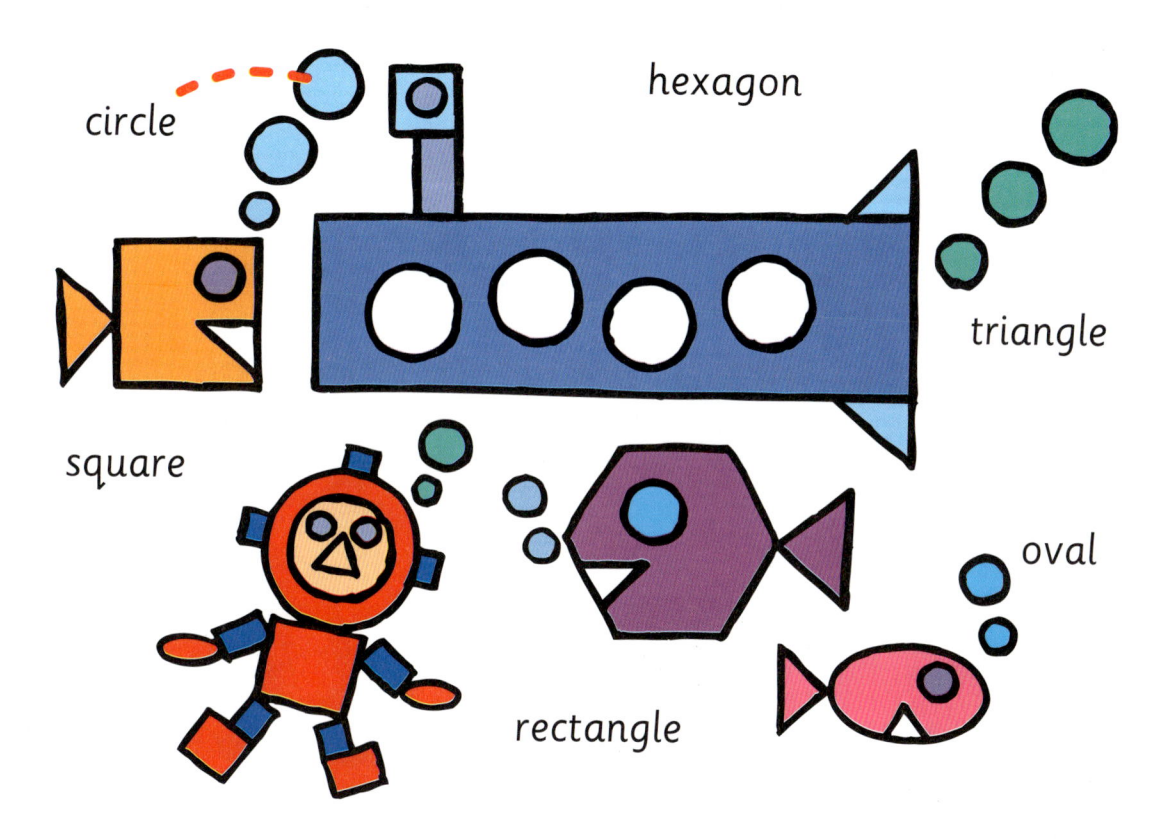

circle

hexagon

triangle

square

oval

rectangle

Answer these questions about the shapes picture. Draw a line under the right word.

What shape is the submarine?

rectangle   square
hexagon

What shape are the bubbles?

circles   ovals
triangles

What shape are the fish tails?

triangles   squares
rectangles

Splendid shapes!

Play this word game. You will need a die and a counter.
Put the counter on start. Shake the die.
If you shake a 1, move one stone along the path.
If you shake a 2, move two stones along the path.
If you shake a 3, move three stones along the path,
and so on.

Which word did you land on first?

Read the word on the stone you land on. Say it out loud.
Say **three more** words beginning with the **same sound** before you throw again. For example, if you land on the word dog, you could say donkey, dad and day.

The scarecrow is wearing lots of funny clothes. Read the words and match them to his clothes by drawing lines.

tie

jacket

hat

glove

scarf

shoe

trousers

boot

belt

Which word is not drawn? Draw it on the scarecrow.

Note for parents: Ask your child to make a list of the clothes s/he is wearing or an outfit made up of favourite clothes.

Read these clothes words, then write the names in the boxes underneath them on the washing line.

socks   jacket   dress   jumper   shorts

Colour the dress green. Draw a red and yellow pattern on the jumper.

Tick the words that describe the picture and cross those that don't.

two socks   ☐   two sacks   ☐

blue shorts   ☐   blue shirt   ☐

ten pegs   ☐   ten pigs   ☐

Read the story of Goldilocks and the Three Bears.

1. Three bears lived in a house in a wood.

2. A little girl called Goldilocks went inside.

3. She ate three bowls of porridge.

4. Goldilocks sat on a very small chair. It broke.

 Greedy Goldilocks!

5. She lay down to sleep on a very small bed.

6. What happened next? Draw a picture.

Answer these questions about the story.
Tick the right words.

Who lived in the house?

three bats ☐   three bears ☐

What did Goldilocks eat?

porridge ☐   pancake ☐

Who did the small chair belong to?

Daddy Bear ☐   Baby Bear ☐

Note for parents: Make sure your child is familiar with traditional folk and fairy stories.

Read the holiday words, then look at the picture.

beach   sea   sun   sand   shell

Choose the words that make the sentences match the picture. Write them in the boxes.

The spade is [ ] the bucket.   in   beside

The bird is on top of the man's [ ] .   head   hand

The crab is [ ] the hat.   under   on

Five [ ] are on the sandcastle.   flags   shells

The [ ] is in the sky.   sea   sun

 Have you ever built a sandcastle?

Jill is going on holiday to a hot place. Read the words.
What should she take? Write them on her list.

sun hat   shorts   sun cream   spade   scarf
T-shirt   towel   bucket   gloves   boots

JILL'S HOLIDAY LIST

Jack is going on holiday
to a cold place.
Cross out the things he
does **not** need.

sun hat   coat
boots   bucket
spade   gloves

Note for parents: This exercise teaches your child to read holiday words and make appropriate choices. Relate the activities to your child's own experiences of visiting different places.

My name is
Greedy Bug.
The thing I like
best is eating.

Choose some food
for me.
Write the words
in the boxes.

For breakfast
I like to eat [   ] .

trees   toast
ties   trains

For lunch
I like to eat [   ] .

beans   bees
books   balls

For dinner
I like to eat [   ] .

coats   chairs
chips   clocks

I like to drink [   ] .

gravy   jam
juice   jelly

Read the clues to solve the puzzles.

I am white.
I come from cows.
You drink me.
What am I?

I am yellow.
I taste sweet.
Bees make me.
What am I?

_____   _____

What do you like eating best?

Read the names of the fruits and vegetables.

| potatoes | pears | peas | cabbage |
| oranges | apples | carrots | bananas |

Some labels are missing. Choose the right words from the list and write them in the space.

Which foods begin with **p**? _____

Which foods begin with **c**?

Which fruit or vegetable do you like best? Draw it and write its name here.

_____

Read the seven days of the week.

Sunday   Monday   Tuesday   Wednesday
Thursday   Friday   Saturday

Read Tim's diary. Write the missing words in the boxes. Choose from this list.

book   ball   computer   television   dog   swimming   bicycle

On Sunday I read a ☐ .

On Monday I played on my ☐ .

On Tuesday I went ☐ .

On Wednesday I took my ☐ for a walk.

On Thursday I played ☐ .

On Friday I went for a ride on my ☐ .

On Saturday I watched ☐ .

Note for parents: This introduces the days of the week and the seasons words. Look at a calendar or diary with your child and explain how it works.

Read the four seasons of the year.

| spring | summer | autumn | winter |

Tick true or false.

It is warm in winter.   true ☐   false ☐

Snow falls in summer.   true ☐   false ☐

Summer comes after spring.   true ☐   false ☐

The spring flowers have three petals.
Colour the summer flowers blue.

The summer leaves are still on the tree. Colour the autumn leaves brown. The winter tree has no leaves.

In which season is your birthday?

Read the animal words.

cow   horse   sheep   dog   cat   hen

Read the words of Old MacDonald, then sing the song.

Old MacDonald had a farm,
E – I – E – I – O.
And on that farm he had a **cow**,
E – I – E – I – O.
With a **moo moo** here,
And a **moo moo** there,
Here a **moo**, there a **moo**,
Everywhere a **moo moo**.
Old MacDonald had a farm,
E – I – E – I – O.

Sing the song again.
Choose a different farm animal each time.

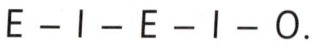

Super duper singing!

Write the noises the animals make in the speech bubbles.

cluck   quack

miaow   baa   woof

sheep

hen

duck

dog

cat

buzz

Draw and colour the animal that makes this noise.

cow   kid

horse   puppy

goat   calf

cat   foal

dog   kitten

Draw lines to match the names of the animals to the names of the babies.

Read the clues to help you solve the puzzles.

I have eight legs.
I spin a web.
What am I?

spider ✓

I have long ears.
I have a fluffy tail.
I live in a burrow.
What am I?

Draw lines from the fishing rods to things that live in water.

eel

shark

moth

lion

seal

octopus

mole

Brilliant work, choose a star!

Class Two made an animal chart. Help them fill it in. Put a tick in the right boxes.

	bat ✓	frog	snail ✓	crab	swan ✓
It has wings.	bat ✓ ✓				
It can swim.	frog				
It has a shell.	snail ✓				
It can fly.	swan ✓				
It moves slowly.	crab ✓				

worm	polar bear	whale
lion	grizzly bear	monkey
tiger	teddy bear	shark

Class Two are using information books in the library. The books are in alphabetical order. Can you write the missing letters on the books?

Which books should the children look in to find out about these things? Draw lines to match the pictures to the books.

alligators

dinosaurs

elephants

helicopters

 Note for parents: Visit a library or book shop with your child and look at non-fiction books together.

Here are some story books. The titles are mixed up.

Draw lines to match the two parts of each book title.

Alice in	Billy Goats Gruff
Jack and the	Wonderland
The Ugly	Beanstalk
The Three	Riding Hood
Little Red	Duckling

Tick the title if it matches the picture on the book.

Puss in Boots ☐

 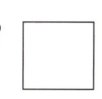

The Little Red Hen ☐

Draw pictures for these books.

Old Brown Bear

The Happy Dragon

This is a poster all about the school show.

Tick the right answers to these questions.

What date is the school show?	10th June ☐	10th July ☐
What day is the show?	Thursday ☐	Friday ☐
What time does it start?	1pm ☐	4pm ☐
How much are tickets for children?	10p ☐	25p ☐

Note for parents: This exercise tests reading accuracy and comprehension. Look at signs, notices or posters when you are out with your child.

1. Jill was in the school band.

2. Her baby brother Lee came to watch.

3. Lee lost his balloon. It went on to the stage.

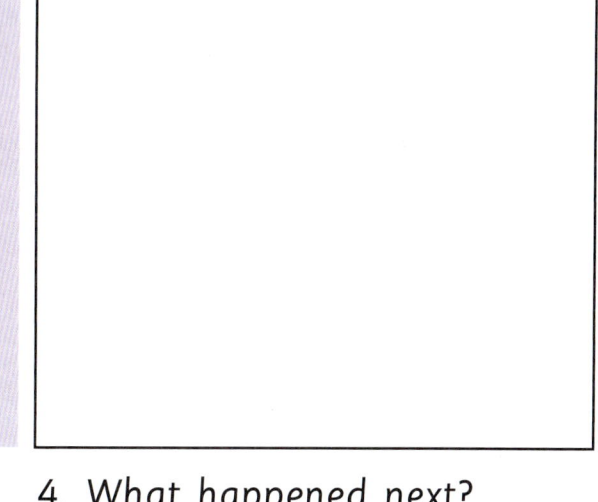

4. What happened next? Draw the picture.

The children are playing in the park.

Choose the right word to finish each sentence and write them in the boxes.

Ben [ ] his bike.   sits   rolls   rides

Jenny [ ] on one leg.   hips   sits   hops

Jim [ ] in the sand.   digs   big   dogs

Tick the right words.

Which word is fast?   walk [ ]   run [ ]

Which word is slow?   crawl [ ]   race [ ]

Which word is loud?   shout [ ]   talk [ ]

Which of these words can you do?

Note for parents: This exercise introduces verbs and tests your child's reasoning skills. Write a list of verbs s/he can do and add to it as your child learns new skills.

Here is a wall of bricks. Some of the words on the bricks rhyme. They sound the same, like **leg** and **peg**.

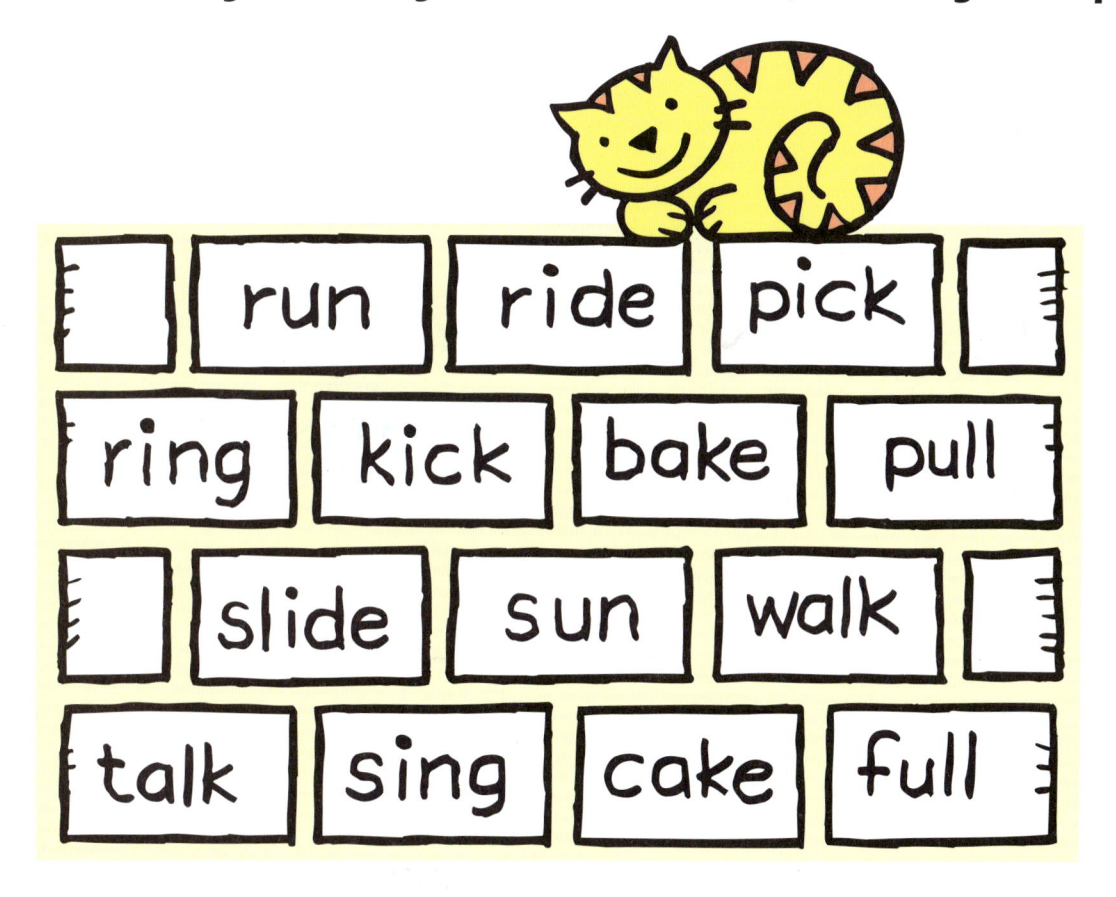

	run	ride	pick	
ring	kick	bake	pull
	slide	sun	walk	
talk	sing	cake	full

Find another word that rhymes with the words in this list.

ride	Colour both word bricks red.
bake	Colour both word bricks yellow.
kick	Colour both word bricks blue.
full	Colour both word bricks green.

Choose colours for the other sets of word bricks that rhyme.

Note for parents: Reading and matching rhyming words builds an awareness of rhyme, which helps when learning to spell.

The garage is a busy place. Some of the signs are empty. Choose words and write them on the signs.

IN   OUT

no smoking   SHOP   car wash

Note for parents: Help your child look for and read signs and words when you go out together.